THE POCKET BOOK OF IRISH
PRAYERS
& BLESSINGS

Gill Books
Hume Avenue, Park West, Dublin 12

www.gillbooks.ie

Gill Books is an imprint of M.H. Gill & Co.

ISBN 9780717189915

This book was created and produced by Teapot Press Ltd

Edited by Fiona Biggs
Designed by Tony Potter

Printed in Europe

This book is typeset in Garamond.

5 4 3 2 1

The Pocket Book of Irish PRAYERS & BLESSINGS

Gill Books

Contents

INTRODUCTION

We can pray anywhere – no special place is required, no particular words are compulsory, except in communal settings, where people are praying aloud. We can pray privately at home, at work, while using public transport, when we're standing in a supermarket queue, strolling in the park or cooking dinner. We pray publicly at Mass, at school assemblies, at prayer meetings and retreats.

Prayer is how we develop and maintain an intimate relationship with God, a relationship that will provide us with strength and consolation in times of difficulty.

Prayer can take many forms – a quick grace before meals, a family Rosary, a meditation on the

MAY the beauty of God
be reflected in your eyes,
the love of God
be reflected in your hands,
the wisdom of God
be reflected in your words,
and the knowledge of God
flow from your heart,
that all might see,
and seeing, believe.

MAY God's Spirit surround you,
and those whom you love.
Rest now, in that calm embrace,
let your hearts be warmed
and all storms be stilled
by the whisper of his voice.

words of Scripture, a prayer of intercession to the Mother of God or a favourite saint for a special intention. Any dialogue that we have with God or his saints is prayer.

This book provides a collection of prayers and blessings for every occasion, from seasonal celebrations during the liturgical year, such as Christmas and Easter, to prayers for the dying, the Serenity Prayer, intercessory prayers to favourite saints, including the Little Flower, St Christopher, St Francis and St Anthony, and blessings for weddings, new babies and the family home.

As you turn the pages you'll realise that many of prayers are familiar to you – and perhaps there'll be a few that are new to you that you can add to your list of favourites.

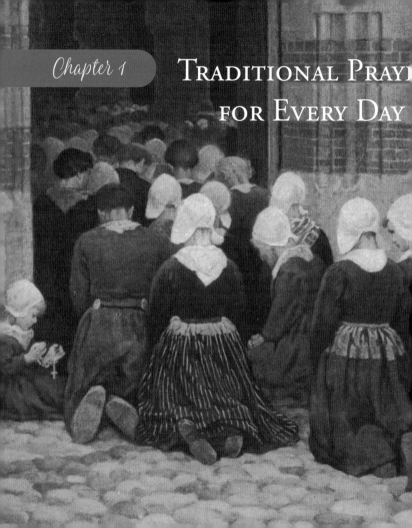

Chapter 1

TRADITIONAL PRAYERS
for Every Day

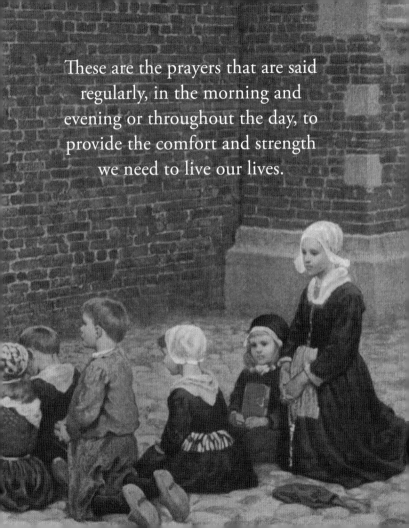

These are the prayers that are said regularly, in the morning and evening or throughout the day, to provide the comfort and strength we need to live our lives.

Sign of the Cross

IN the name of the
Father,
and of the Son,
and of the Holy
Spirit. Amen.

Our Father

Our Father, who art in heaven,
hallowed be thy name.
Thy kingdom come,
thy will be done,
on earth, as it is in heaven.
Give us this day our
daily bread
and forgive us our trespasses as we
forgive those who trespass against us;
and lead us
not into temptation,
but deliver us from evil. Amen.

Hail Mary

HAIL Mary,
Full of Grace,
The Lord is with thee.
Blessed art thou among women,
and blessed is the fruit
of thy womb, Jesus.

Holy Mary,
Mother of God,
pray for us sinners now,
and at the hour of our death. Amen.

Glory Be to the Father

GLORY be to the Father,
and to the Son,
and to the Holy Spirit.
As it was in the beginning, is now,
and ever shall be,
world without end. Amen.

Apostles' Creed

I BELIEVE in God,
the Father almighty,
Creator of heaven and earth,
and in Jesus Christ, his only Son, our Lord,
who was conceived by the Holy Spirit,
born of the Virgin Mary,
suffered under Pontius Pilate,
was crucified, died and was buried;
he descended into hell;
on the third day he rose again from the dead;
he ascended into heaven,
and is seated at the right hand of God the Father almighty;
from there he will come to judge the living and the dead.
I believe in the Holy Spirit,
the holy catholic Church,
the communion of saints,
the forgiveness of sins,
the resurrection of the body,
and life everlasting. Amen.

Prayer to the Holy Spirit

Come Holy Spirit, fill the hearts of your faithful and kindle in them the fire of your love. Send forth your Spirit and they shall be created. And you shall renew the face of the earth.

O, God, who by the light of the Holy Spirit, did instruct the hearts of the faithful, grant that by the same Holy Spirit we may be truly wise and ever enjoy his consolations, Through Christ our Lord, Amen.

A woman kneels in prayer at a Pietà at Sheep's Head near Ahakista, County Cork.

The Serenity Prayer

GOD grant me the serenity
To accept the things I cannot change;
Courage to change the things I can;
And wisdom to know the difference.
Living one day at a time;
Enjoying one moment at a time;
Accepting hardships as the pathway to peace;
Taking, as God did, this sinful world
As it is, not as I would have it;
Trusting that he will make things right
If I surrender to his will;
So that I may be reasonably happy in this life
And supremely happy with him
For ever and ever in the next. Amen.

Guardian Angel Prayer

ANGEL of God,
my guardian dear,
To whom God's love
commits me here,
Ever this day,
be at my side,
to light and guard,
to rule and guide. Amen.

Grace Before Meals

Bless us, O Lord,
and these thy gifts,
which of your bounty
we are about to receive,
through Christ our Lord. Amen.

Chapter 2

MARY

Harry Clarke stained-glass window in the Church of the Nativity of the Blessed Virgin Mary at Timoleague, County Cork.

There has always
been great devotion
in Ireland to Mary,
the Mother of God.
For a long time
there was a tradition
that the eldest girl in
a family was given
the name Mary,
or one of its many
variants. The Hail
Mary is one of our
daily prayers, and
the nightly Rosary
is a regular event in
many homes.

The Memorare

REMEMBER, O most gracious Virgin Mary,
that never was it known that anyone
who fled to thy protection,
implored thy help, or sought thy intercession
was left unaided.
Inspired with this confidence,
I fly to thee, O Virgin of virgins, my Mother;
to thee do I come; before thee I stand,
sinful and sorrowful.
O Mother of the Word Incarnate,
despise not my petitions,
but in thy mercy hear and answer me. Amen.

The Magnificat

My soul magnifies the Lord,
and my spirit rejoices in God my Saviour,
for he has looked with favour on the lowliness of his
servant.
Surely, from now on all generations will call me blessed;
for the Mighty One has done great things for me,
and holy is his name.
His mercy is for those who fear him
from generation to generation.
He has shown strength with his arm;
he has scattered the proud in the thoughts of their hearts.
He has brought down the powerful from their thrones,
and lifted up the lowly;
he has filled the hungry with good things,
and sent the rich away empty.
He has helped his servant Israel,
in remembrance of his mercy,
according to the promise he made to our ancestors,
to Abraham and to his descendants for ever. Amen.

Prayer to Our Lady of Knock

OUR Lady of Knock, Queen of Ireland,
you gave hope to our people in a time of distress
and comforted them in sorrow.
You have inspired countless pilgrims
to pray with confidence to your divine Son,
remembering his promise:
'Ask and you shall receive,
Seek and you shall find'.
Help me to remember
that we are all pilgrims on the road to heaven.
Fill me with love and concern
for my brothers and sisters in Christ,
especially those who live with me.
Comfort me when I am sick
or lonely or depressed. Teach me how to take part
ever more reverently in the holy Mass.
Pray for me now, and at the hour of my death. Amen.

Ireland's National Marian Shrine,
Knock, County Mayo.

Prayer to Our Lady of Lourdes

O EVER immaculate virgin, Mother of Mercy,
Health of the sick,
Refuge of sinners,
Comfort of the afflicted,
You know my needs, my troubles, my sufferings;
Cast on me a look of pity.

By appearing in the grotto of Lourdes
You were pleased to make it a privileged sanctuary,
From which you dispense your favours,
And already many sufferers have obtained the cure of
their infirmities,
Both spiritual and physical.

I come, therefore,
With the most unbounded confidence,
To implore your maternal intercession.
Obtain, most loving mother, my requests,
Through Jesus Christ, your son, our Lord. Amen.

Hail, Holy Queen (Salve Regina)

Hail, holy Queen, Mother of mercy,
hail our life, our sweetness and our hope.
To thee do we cry, poor banished children of Eve:
to thee do we send up our sighs,
mourning and weeping in this valley of tears.
Turn then, most gracious Advocate,
thine eyes of mercy towards us,
and after this our exile,
show unto us the blessed fruit of thy womb, Jesus.
O clement, O loving, O sweet Virgin Mary! Amen.

The Miraculous Medal Prayer

O Mary, conceived without sin,
pray for us who have recourse to you.
May this medal be a sign
of your love for us
And a witness of our devotion to you. Amen.

SALVE·REGINA

St John Henry Newman's Prayer to Mary

O MOTHER of Jesus, and my Mother, let me dwell
with you,
cling to you and love you with ever-increasing love.
I promise the honour, love and trust of a child.
Give me a mother's protection, for I need your
watchful care.
You know better than any other the thoughts and desires
of the Sacred Heart.
Keep constantly before my mind the same thoughts, the
same desires, that my heart may be filled with zeal for the
interests of the Sacred Heart of your Divine Son.
Instill in me a love of all that is noble, that I may no
longer be easily turned to selfishness.
Help me, dearest Mother, to acquire the virtues that God
wants of me: to forget myself always, to work solely for
him, without fear of sacrifice. I shall always rely on your
help to be what Jesus wants me to be.
I am his; I am yours, my good Mother!
Give me each day your holy and maternal blessing until

my last evening on earth,
when your Immaculate Heart will present me to the
heart of Jesus in heaven,
there to love and bless you and your divine Son for all
eternity. Amen.

The Litany of Loreto

LORD, have mercy.

Christ, have mercy.

Lord, have mercy.

God our Father ln Heaven, have mercy on us.

God the Son, Redeemer of the world, have mercy on us.

God the Holy Spirit, have mercy on us.

Holy Trinity, one God, have mercy on us.

Holy Mary, pray for us.

Holy Mother of God, pray for us.

Most honored of virgins, pray for us.

Mother of Christ, pray for us.

Mother of the Church, pray for us.

Mother of divine grace, pray for us.

Mother most pure, pray for us.

Mother of chaste love, pray for us.

Mother and virgin, pray for us.

Sinless Mother, pray for us.

Dearest of Mothers, pray for us.

Model of motherhood, pray for us.

Mother of good counsel, pray for us.

Mother of our Creator, pray for us.

Mother of our Saviour, pray for us.

Virgin most wise, pray for us.

Virgin rightly praised, pray for us.

Virgin rightly renowned, pray for us.

Virgin most powerful, pray for us.

Virgin gentle in mercy, pray for us.

Faithful Virgin, pray for us.

Mirror of justice, pray for us.

Throne of wisdom, pray for us.

Cause of our joy, pray for us.

Shrine of the Spirit, pray for us.

Glory of Israel, pray for us.

Vessel of selfless devotion, pray for us.

Mystical Rose, pray for us.

Tower of David, pray for us.

Tower of ivory, pray for us.

House of gold, pray for us.

Ark of the covenant, pray for us.

Gate of heaven, pray for us.

Morning star, pray for us.
Health of the sick, pray for us.
Refuge of sinners, pray for us.
Comfort of the troubled, pray for us.
Help of Christians, pray for us.
Queen of angels, pray for us.
Queen of patriarchs and prophets, pray for us.
Queen of apostles and martyrs, pray for us.
Queen of confessors and virgins, pray for us.
Queen of all saints, pray for us.
Queen conceived without sin, pray for us.
Queen assumed into heaven, pray for us.
Queen of the Rosary, pray for us.
Queen of families, pray for us.
Queen of peace, pray for us.
Blessed be the name of the Virgin Mary
now and for ever. Amen.

The Angelus

THE Angel of the Lord declared unto Mary,
And she conceived of the Holy Spirit.

Hail Mary,
Full of Grace,
The Lord is with thee.
Blessed art thou among women,
and blessed is the fruit
of thy womb, Jesus.

Holy Mary,
Mother of God,
pray for us sinners now,
and at the hour of our death.

Behold the handmaid of the Lord.
Be it done unto me according to Your Word.

Hail Mary, etc. …

And the Word was made flesh,
And dwelt among us.

Hail Mary, etc. …

Pray for us, O holy Mother of God.
That we may be made worthy of the promises of Christ.

Pour forth, we beseech You, O Lord,
Your Grace into our hearts;
that as we have known the incarnation of Christ,
your Son by the message of an angel,
so by his passion and cross
we may be brought to the glory of his Resurrection.
Through the same Christ, our Lord. Amen.

The Rosary

The Rosary originates from the 13th century, with an apparition of the Blessed Virgin Mary to St Dominic. She asked him to institute a way of praying the Our Father, Hail Mary and Glory Be to the Father, as a replacement for praying the Psalms. Dominic's rosary had 15 decades.

The nightly family Rosary is a long-standing tradition in Ireland, although it is also popular for private, personal prayer. The standard five-decade pair of rosary beads has five groups of ten beads, each group separated by a larger bead. Each Rosary focuses on one of four sets of mysteries (there are five mysteries in each set): The Joyful Mysteries; The Luminous Mysteries (added by Pope St John Paul II in 2002); The Sorrowful Mysteries; the Glorious Mysteries.

The Apostles' Creed (see page 18) is said while holding the crucifix; an Our Father is said on the first large bead next to the crucifix, then a Hail Mary on each of the next three beads, and a Glory Be to the Father on the chain. If you are praying the Rosary in a group, the leader then announces the first mystery. (If you are praying alone, meditate silently on each mystery.) Say one Our Father on the next large bead, then say one Hail Mary on each bead in the first decade, while meditating on the mystery, and finish with a Glory Be to the Father on the chain. Repeat for the remaining four mysteries, saying an Our Father on the larger bead in between each decade.

The Mysteries

1. The Five Joyful Mysteries are said on Mondays and Saturday, and on Sundays from Advent until Lent. We meditate on the time during which the birth of Jesus was anticipated, and on his early years.

First Joyful Mystery: The Annunciation

Second Joyful Mystery: The Visitation

Third Joyful Mystery: The Birth of Jesus

Fourth Joyful Mystery: The Presentation of Jesus in the Temple

Fifth Joyful Mystery: The Finding of Jesus in the Temple

2. The Five Luminous Mysteries are said on Thursdays (except during Lent). We meditate on the public ministry of Jesus, the period during which he announced the coming of the kingdom of God.

First Luminous Mystery: Jesus' Baptism in the River Jordan

Second Luminous Mystery: Jesus' Miracle at Cana

Third Luminous Mystery: Jesus' Proclamation of the Kingdom

Fourth Luminous Mystery: The Transfiguration of Our Lord

Fifth Luminous Mystery: Jesus' Institution of the Eucharist

3. The Five Sorrowful Mysteries are said on Tuesdays and Fridays, and every day from Ash Wednesday until Easter Sunday. We meditate on the events surrounding the end of Jesus' earthly life, his sacrifice so that we might be redeemed.

First Sorrowful Mystery: The Agony in the Garden

Second Sorrowful Mystery: The Scourging at the Pillar

Third Sorrowful Mystery: The Crowning with Thorns

Fourth Sorrowful Mystery: The Carrying of the Cross

Fifth Sorrowful Mystery: The Crucifixion

4. The Five Glorious Mysteries are said on Wednesdays (except during Lent) and on Sundays from Easter until Advent. We meditate on Christ's sacrifice on the cross, through which we achieve our redemption.

First Glorious Mystery: The Resurrection

Second Glorious Mystery: The Ascension

Third Glorious Mystery: The Descent of the Holy Spirit

Fourth Glorious Mystery: The Assumption

Fifth Glorious Mystery: The Coronation of Mary, Queen of Heaven

Concluding Prayer

O GOD, whose only-begotten son, by his life, death and resurrection, has purchased for us the rewards of eternal life: grant, we beseech you, that, meditating upon these mysteries of the most holy Rosary of the Blessed Virgin Mary, we may imitate what they contain and obtain what they promise, through the same Christ our Lord. Amen.

Chapter 3

Praying with the Saints

We pray to our favourite
saints, using their own
words, or those of others,
for intercession with God
when we are in need.

St Bernadette (16 April)

Bernadette Soubirous was born in southern France in 1844. In 1858, she said that she had been seeing, at a grotto at Lourdes, an apparition of 'a young lady', who had identified herself as 'the Immaculate Conception'. A canonical investigation upheld her claims and the apparition was named Our Lady of Lourdes. The grotto became an international shrine, with millions of visitors annually. Bernadette joined the Sisters of Charity at Nevers. She died of tuberculosis in 1879 and was canonised in 1925. She is the patron saint of people who are ridiculed for their beliefs.

St Bernadette's Prayer

GRANT me the grace to see your hand in my affliction,
And to desire no other comforter but you.

Prayer to St Bernadette

ST BERNADETTE, pure and simple child,
You were privileged to behold the beauty
Of Mary Immaculate
and to be the recipient of her confidence 18 times at Lourdes;
You who did desire from then on to hide yourself in the cloister of Nevers
And there live and die as a victim of sinners,
Obtain for us that spirit of purity, simplicity and mortification
That will lead us also to the glorious vision
Of God and Mary in Heaven. Amen.

St Blaise (3 February)

St Blaise lived in Armenia in the fourth century. He once saved a child who was choking on a fish bone and is revered as the patron saint of those afflicted with throat ailments. On his feast day many churches have a ceremony for the blessing of throats.

Prayer to St Blaise

O GLORIOUS St Blaise, by your martyrdom you left to the Church a precious witness to the faith. Obtain for us the grace to preserve within ourselves this divine gift, and to defend, both by word and example, the truth of that same faith, which is so wickedly attacked and slandered in our times. You who miraculously restored a little child when it was at the point of death by reason of an affliction of the throat, grant us thy mighty protection in like misfortunes; and, above all, obtain for us the grace of Christian mortification together with a faithful observance of the precepts of the Church, which may keep us from offending Almighty God. Amen.

St Brendan (16 May)

St Brendan was born in 484 in Tralee, County Kerry. He studied under St Jarlath at Tuam and St Finnian at Clonard, and is regarded as one of the Apostles of Ireland. He founded several monasteries, most notably Ardfert and Clonfert, where he was buried. In 512, with 14 companions, he embarked from the foot of Mount Brandon on a seven-year voyage to find the Isles of the Blessed. He died in 577 and is the patron of Kerry, sailors and whales. His short prayer, 'Lord, protect me, for the sea is so vast, and I am so small', can be used in situations where we feel at the mercy of events beyond our control.

Prayer of St Brendan the Navigator

HELP me to journey beyond the familiar
and into the unknown.
Give me the faith to leave old ways
and break fresh ground with you.
Christ of the mysteries, I trust you

to be stronger than each storm within me.
I will trust in the darkness and know
that my times, even now, are in your hand.
Tune my spirit to the music of heaven,
and somehow, make my obedience count for you. Amen.

St Brigid (1 February)

St Brigid of Kildare is one of Ireland's three patron saints. She was born in Dundalk in 450 into a noble family, but resisted the strategic marriage that was expected of a woman of her station. She took the veil and founded several convents. Several miracles were attributed to her during her lifetime, and she designed the cross that is named after her and is still placed above the threshold in Irish homes to protect all within. Brigid is the patron saint of Ireland, babies, midwives, scholars, poets and travellers. She died in 523.

Brigid wove a cross from rushes to teach a dying pagan chieftain about Christianity. The cross is still displayed above the door in Irish homes to invoke Brigid's protection.

Prayer to St Brigid

You were a woman of peace.
You brought harmony where there was conflict.
You brought light to the darkness.
You brought hope to the downcast.
May the mantle of your peace cover those who are
troubled and anxious, and may peace be firmly rooted in
our hearts and in our world.
Inspire us to act justly and to reverence all God has made.

Brigid, you were a voice for
the wounded and the weary.
Strengthen what is weak
within us.
Calm us into a quietness that
heals and listens.
May we grow each day into
greater wholeness in mind,
body and spirit.
Amen.

Blessing of St Brigid's Crosses

Father of all creation and Lord of Light,
you have given us life and entrusted your creation to us
to use it and to care for it.
We ask you to bless these crosses made of green rushes in
memory of holy Brigid,
who used the cross to recall and to teach your Son's life,
death and resurrection.
May these crosses be a sign of our sharing in the Paschal
Mystery of your Son and a sign of your protection of
our lives, our land and its creatures through Brigid's
intercession during the coming year and always. We ask
this through Christ our Lord.
The crosses are sprinkled with holy water:
May the blessing of God, Father, Son and Holy Spirit be
on these crosses and on the places where they hang and
on everyone who looks at them. Amen.

St Anthony of Padua (13 June)

One of the church's most popular saints, St Anthony of Padua was a Portuguese priest who joined the Franciscans and became one of the order's most powerful preachers and missioners, travelling throughout France and Italy. He was renowned for his holiness and achieved a reputation as a powerful intercessor with God. He is a very relatable saint and is usually depicted with the Christ child in his arms, or holding his symbol, the lily, or both. He died in 1231 at the age of 36, and was canonised by Pope Gregory IX at Spoleto Cathedral the following year. He is the patron saint of those who have lost things.

Prayer to St Anthony to Recover Lost Things

O BLESSED St Anthony
God's grace has made you a powerful advocate in all our needs
and the patron for the restoration of things lost or stolen.
I turn to you today with childlike love and deep confidence.
You have helped countless children of God
to find the things they have lost, material things, and, more importantly,
the things of the spirit: Faith, hope and love.
I come to you with confidence;
help me in my present need.
I recommend what I have lost to your care,
in the hope that God will restore it to me,
if it is his holy will. Amen.

St Christopher (25 July)

St Christopher (whose name means Christbearer) is said to have carried the Christ-child across a raging river. He found his burden very heavy because the Child had the weight of the world on his shoulders. He is a popular saint, the patron of all travellers. Many people wear a St Christopher medal for protection from danger.

Prayer to St Christopher

TEACH us to be true Christ-bearers,
carrying the Good News to all who do not know Jesus.
Protect us as we travel through the world
on our pilgrimage to our Father in heaven.
Through Christ our lord. Amen.

St Clare of Assisi (11 August)

St Clare, born in Assisi in 1194, was one of the first followers of St Francis. She founded the order of Poor Ladies, now known as the Poor Clares. Her order followed the very strict rule of St Francis – the sisters slept on the floor, ate no meat and spent their days in silence, working and praying. Clare came under a lot of pressure to modify her harsh rule, but, recognising her determination, the pope absolved her of any requirement to do so. She died in 1253 and was canonised in 1255. She is the patron of television and people suffering from eye disease.

Prayer to St Clare for Healing

O Blessed Saint Clare,
your life shines like a beacon
and cast its light down the ages of the Church
to guide the way of Christ.

Look with compassion on the poor and humble
who call on you for help.
As you bow before your Eucharistic Lord in heaven,
speak to him of my afflicted body and my broken spirit.
Ask him to heal me and to wash away my sins
in his precious blood.
Great Servant of Christ,
remember the needs of my family
and all those I pray for. Amen.

ST COLUMBA

St Columba (9 June)

St Columba, patron saint of Derry and of Ireland, was
born in Donegal in 521. He established his first monastery
at Derry in 548. In 553 he travelled to the island of Iona,
off the coast of Scotland, with 12 monks, and founded his
famous monastery there. He died on Iona in 597. Columba
is also known as St Columcille.

St Columba's Prayer

BE a bright flame before me, God,
a guiding star above me.
Be a smooth path before me,
a kindly shepherd behind me
Today, tonight and for ever,
alone with none but you my God,
I journey on my way;
What need I fear when you are near,
O Lord of night and day?
I'm more secure within your hand
than if a multitude around me stands. Amen.

St Francis of Assisi (4 October)

Francis was the founder of the Franciscan order. Born in 1182, at the age of 20 he dedicated himself to God and embraced a life of poverty. He died in 1226 and was canonised two years later. His love of animals and nature is recognised in his designation as patron of animals and the environment. The Peace Prayer, attributed to Francis, is one of our most popular prayers.

St Francis's Morning Prayer

LORD, help me to live this day, quietly, easily;
to lean on your great strength, trustfully, respectfully;
to wait for the unfolding of your will, patiently, serenely;
to meet others, peacefully, joyfully;
to face tomorrow, confidently, courageously. Amen.

The Peace Prayer of St Francis

LORD, make me an instrument of your peace:
where there is hatred, let me sow love;
where there is injury, pardon;
where there is doubt, faith;
where there is despair, hope;
where there is darkness, light;
where there is sadness, joy.

O divine Master, grant that I may not so much seek
to be consoled as to console,
to be understood as to understand,
to be loved as to love.
For it is in giving that we receive,
it is in pardoning that we are pardoned,
and it is in dying that we are born to eternal life. Amen.

St Francis Xavier (3 December)

One of the founders of the Jesuit order, St Francis Xavier was born in Spain in 1506. He was ordained in 1537 and devoted his life to spreading the Gospel. He spearheaded successful missions in Goa, India, and in Japan and is said to have baptised 30,000 people. He died in 1552, while awaiting permission to enter China to continue his missionary work. He was canonised in 1622 and is the patron saint of missionaries.

Prayer to St Francis Xavier

GREAT St Francis,
Beloved and full of charity,
in union with you I adore the Divine Majesty.
I give thanks to God for the singular gifts of grace
bestowed on you in life and of glory after death,
and I beg of you, with all the affection of my heart,
by your powerful intercession
obtain for me the grace to live a holy life and die a
holy death.
I beg you to obtain for me (*mention your petition*).
But if what I ask is not for the glory of God and for
my wellbeing,
obtain for me, I beseech you,
what will more certainly attain these ends.
Through Christ our Lord. Amen.

St Gerard Majella (16 October)

Gerard Majella, patron saint of mothers-to-be, was born
in Italy in 1726. In 1749 he joined the Redemptorists as
a lay brother and worked to support the poor and needy.
Many miracles were attributed to him. A young woman
who had come into possession of his handkerchief
was dying in childbirth. After she had asked for his
handkerchief to be brought to her she was safely
delivered of a healthy child. Gerard Majella died in 1755
and was canonised in 1904.

An Expectant Mother's Prayer to St Gerard

DEAR St Gerard,
you were especially sensitive to the needs of mothers.
Pray for me and my baby.
Ask our good Lord to keep us happy and safe,
and bring us to a joyful birth. Amen.

Pope St John XXIII (11 October)

Known as the 'Good Pope', John XXIII's short reign lasted from 1958 to 1963. He died in the middle of the Second Vatican Council (1962–65), which he had called to instigate reform in the Church. He was canonised in 2014. He was passionate about equality: 'We were all made in God's image, and thus, we are all Godly alike.'

Pope St John XXIII's Prayer for Strength

EVERY day I need you, Lord, but today especially,
I need some extra strength to face whatever is to come.
This day, more than any other day,
I need to feel you near me to strengthen my courage
and to overcome any fear.
By myself I cannot meet the challenge of the hour.
We are frail human creatures and we need a higher power
to sustain us in all that life may bring.
And so, dear Lord, hold my trembling hand.
Be with me, Lord, this day,
and stretch out your powerful arms to help me.
May your love be upon me as I place all my hope in you.
Amen.

St John Henry Newman (9 October)

One of the most recent additions to the ranks of sainthood, John Henry Newman was born in London in 1801. He was ordained to the Anglican priesthood, but later converted to Catholicism and was made a cardinal. He lived in Dublin for a number of years and established the Catholic University there. Two miracles having been attributed to him, he was canonised in 2019.

Prayer of St John Henry Newman

MAY the Lord support us
all the day long,
till the shades lengthen and the
evening comes,
and the busy world is hushed,
and the fever of life is over,
and our work is done.
Then in his mercy
may he give us a safe lodging,
and holy rest,
and peace at the last. Amen.

Pope St John Paul II (22 October)

Cardinal Karol Wojtyła, born in Poland in 1920, was elected to the papacy in 1978, taking the name John Paul II, in honour of his predecessor. He was the first non-Italian pope in almost five centuries and had one of the longest papal reigns. He travelled widely during his pontificate and worked constantly to improve relations between Catholicism and the other world religions. He died in 2005, and was canonised in 2014.

Prayer for the intercession of Pope St John Paul II

O Holy Trinity,
we thank you for having given to the Church
Pope John Paul II,
and for having made him shine with your fatherly
tenderness,
the glory of the cross of Christ and the splendour of the
Spirit of love.
He, trusting completely in your infinite mercy
and in the maternal intercession of Mary, has shown
himself
in the likeness of Jesus the Good Shepherd
and has pointed out to us holiness
as the path to reach eternal communion with you.
Grant us, through his intercession,
according to your will, the grace that we implore. Amen.

St Joseph (19 March)

The foster-father of Jesus, St Joseph is revered as the patron of workers, families and the home and is petitioned for the grace of a happy death (he himself had the happiest of deaths, in the arms of Jesus and Mary). St Matthew, in his gospel, describes St Joseph as 'a just man'.

Prayer to St Joseph

O St Joseph, whose protection is so great, so strong, so prompt before the throne of God, I place in you all my interests and desires.

Assist me by your powerful intercession and obtain for me from your divine son all spiritual blessings through Jesus Christ, our Lord; so that having engaged here below your heavenly power, I may offer my thanksgiving and homage to the most loving of Fathers.

I never weary contemplating you and Jesus asleep in your arms. I dare not approach while he reposes near your heart. Press him in my name and kiss his fine head for me, and ask him to return the kiss when I draw my dying breath. St Joseph, patron of departing souls, pray for us. Amen.

St Jude (28 October)

St Jude was one of the 12 Apostles, the son of James. After Jesus' death, he preached the Gospel in the Middle East, and is believed to have been martyred in Beirut (then in Syria) in the year 65. Venerated as the patron of those with 'lost causes', he is a very popular saint and there is great devotion to him in Ireland.

Prayer to St Jude for the Resolution of a Hopeless Case

DEAR St Jude,
Apostle and friend of Jesus,
the Church honours and invokes you
as the patron of hopeless cases.

Pray for me. I implore you to bring visible help
 in my trials and tribulations,
particularly (*make your request*).

I promise to honour you as my special patron
and to encourage devotion to you. Amen.

St Kevin (3 June)

St Kevin is believed to have been born into a noble family in Leinster around 498, and reputedly died in 618 aged 120. He founded a monastery at Glendalough and was its first abbot. He was renowned for his asceticism and his protection of animals. There is a legend that a blackbird laid an egg in Kevin's hand and he kept it outstretched until the chick had hatched. He was canonised in 1903 and is a patron of Dublin and of blackbirds.

Prayer to St Kevin

SAINT Kevin, you were privileged to live in the Age of Saints,
baptised by one saint, taught by another and buried by a third.
We celebrate your saintly and holy life.
You lived a life filled with a wonderful
reverence and awe of all living things.
Let us imitate the respect and appreciation
you showed towards life in all its forms, and
to see the presence of God in all his creations.
We pray that God will one day raise up saints in our day
to help, support and guide us into the way of salvation. Amen.

St Laurence O'Toole (14 November)

This patron saint of Dublin was born in Kildare in 1128. In 1162 Laurence became the first Irish Archbishop of the city of Dublin. Laurence was tireless in his efforts to protect the people of Dublin and throughout the rest of his life he attempted to broker a peace between the kings of Ireland and England. He died in 1180 in Normandy, and was canonised in 1225. His heart is preserved in Christ Church Cathedral, Dublin.

Prayer to St Laurence O'Toole

DEAR St Laurence,
you worked tirelessly in the cause of peace.
Grant us the gifts of tirelessness and
steadfastness as
we try to live our lives as instruments
of the peace, love and tolerance of
Jesus Christ. Amen.

St Mary Magdalene (22 July)

Mary Magdalene was one of Jesus' disciples. She was present at his crucifixion and was the first person to whom he appeared after his resurrection. In 2016 her memorial was raised to the level of feast by Pope Francis, which means that she is now celebrated at the same level as the male apostles. She is prayed to for help in childbirth and by those who are in prison.

Prayer to St Mary Magdalene

St Mary Magdalene,
who by conversion became beloved of Jesus,
we give thanks for your witness to
the forgiveness of Jesus through the miracle of love.

Please intercede for me,
so that I may some day share
in your eternal happiness in his glorious presence. Amen.

St Michael the Archangel (29 September)

St Michael appears in the Old Testament and is revered in the Catholic Church as the Enemy of Satan and the Guardian of the Church. He is the patron of grocers, sailors, police officers and soldiers.

Prayer to St Michael

St Michael the Archangel,
defend us in battle.
Be our protection against the
wickedness and snares of the devil.
May God rebuke him, we humbly pray,
and do you, O Prince of the Heavenly Host,
by the power of God,
cast into hell Satan and all evil spirits
who prowl about the world
seeking the ruin of souls. Amen.

St Oliver Plunkett (11 July)

St Oliver Plunkett was born in Oldcastle, County Meath, in 1625 and was consecrated Archbishop of Armagh at a time when Catholics were being savagely persecuted. After the discovery of a 'popish plot' in 1678, he was captured in 1679, tried for treason and convicted. He was executed at Tyburn in 1681. His head is preserved at St Peter's Church in Drogheda, County Louth.

Prayer to St Oliver Plunkett

GLORIOUS martyr, St Oliver,
who willingly gave your life for your faith,
help us also to be strong in faith.
Like you, may we be loyal
to the See of Peter.
By your intercession and example
may all hatred and bitterness be banished
from the hearts of Irish men and women.
May the peace of Christ reign in our hearts,
as it did in yours, even at the moment of your death.
Pray for us and for Ireland. Amen.

St Patrick (17 March)

The patron saint and national apostle of Ireland, Patrick was brought from Britain to Ireland as a slave in the fifth century. After six years he escaped, was ordained a priest and later returned to the land of his captivity, in order to bring the Gospel to the people of Ireland. He used the shamrock to explain the concept of the Holy Trinity, and to this day we wear the shamrock on St Patrick's feast day. He is also credited with driving the snakes from Ireland. In 432 he travelled to Cashel to baptise King Aengus, who became Ireland's first Christian ruler.

We recite his famous prayer, known as 'St Patrick's Breastplate', whenever we feel in need of divine protection.

St Patrick's Breastplate

The Rock of Cashel, County Tipperary, also known as Cashel of the Kings and St Patrick's Rock, a historic site associated with Patrick.

I BIND to myself today
God's power to guide me,
God's might to uphold me,
God's wisdom to teach me,
God's eye to watch over me,
God's ear to hear me,
God's word to give me speech,
God's hand to guide me,
God's way to lie before me,
God's shield to shelter me,
God's host to secure me,
against the snares of demons,
against the seductions of vices,
against the lusts of nature,
against everyone who meditates
injury to me,

whether far or near,
whether few or with many.

Christ shield me today
against wounding.
Christ with me, Christ before me, Christ behind me,
Christ in me, Christ beneath me, Christ above me,
Christ on my right, Christ on my left,
Christ when I lie down, Christ when I sit down,
Christ in the heart of everyone who thinks of me,
Christ in the mouth of everyone who speaks of me,
Christ in the eye that sees me,
Christ in the ear that hears me.
I arise today
through the mighty strength
of the Lord of creation. Amen.

St Teresa of Calcutta (5 September)

Mother Teresa of Calcutta was born in Albania in 1910. She entered the Loreto order, but in 1946 she received 'a call within a call' and founded the Missionaries of Charity, an order dedicated to helping the poor in the slums of Calcutta. In 1979 she was awarded the Nobel Prize for Peace. She died in 1997 and was canonised in 2016.

Prayer for the Intercession of St Teresa

DEAR God,
you have given us a beautiful example
of love in action through St Mother Teresa.
In her life she showed us how to follow Jesus by loving
and serving others.
She fed the hungry, cared for the sick and dying and gave
shelter to the homeless.
May we imitate her love and generosity by reaching out
to all those who are needy.
Grant us your grace through her intercession. Amen.

St Thérèse of Lisieux, 'The Little Flower' (1 October)

Thérèse of Lisieux, born in 1873, is one of the most popular saints in the Church calendar. She had a religious vocation from an early age, and made every effort to be holy in the ordinary things of life. She entered the Carmelites when she was 15, and was professed as a nun when she was 17. She had always been frail, and she died of tuberculosis in 1897, when she was 24. She was canonised in 1925, and is a patron of the missions. In 1997 she was declared a Doctor of the Church, one of only three women to be so honoured. Prayer was immensely important to her: 'For me, prayer is a surge of the heart; it is a simple look turned towards heaven, it is a cry of recognition and love, embracing both trial and joy.'

Prayer of Intercession to St Thérèse

ST THÉRÈSE, The Little Flower of Jesus,
please pick a rose from the heavenly garden,
and send it to me with a message of love.
I beg you to obtain for me the favours that I seek.

O Lord, grant us, we pray you,
So to walk in the footsteps
Of your blessed virgin Thérèse
With a humble heart,
That we may receive everlasting
rewards. Amen.

St Vincent de Paul (27 September)

The saint of the poor was born in rural France in 1581. He was ordained a priest in 1600 and rejected a life of ecclesiastical prestige, instead setting up various initiatives to help the poor and needy. He was a co-founder of the Daughters of Charity. More than 400 years later his name is still synonymous with the care of the poor, with Vincent de Paul societies operating worldwide. He was canonised in 1737 and is the patron saint of charities.

Prayer of Intercession to St Vincent

Dear St Vincent, friend of the poor,
through your merciful intercession, obtain help
for the destitute,
relief for the abandoned, solace for the
unfortunate, comfort for the sick
and the grace of preaching the Gospel to the poor.

May your example of charity encourage priests
to work for the salvation of all souls
that the love of Christ may be known to all
people.
We ask this through Christ our Lord. Amen.

Chapter 4

Prayers for Advent and Christmas

Advent, which means 'coming', is the time of joyful anticipation leading up to Christmas. It is the beginning of the Church's liturgical year. At Christmas we celebrate the birth of our Saviour, Jesus Christ.

PRAYERS DURING ADVENT

GOD of hope, who brought love into this world,
be the love that dwells between us.
God of hope, who brought peace into this world,
be the peace that dwells between us.
God of hope, who brought joy into this world,
be the joy that dwells between us.
God of hope, the rock we stand upon,
be the centre, the focus of our lives
always, and particularly this Advent time. Amen.

GOD of hope and promise, be with us throughout
this Advent season and draw us ever closer as we
journey together towards the stable and the birth
of your Son, our Saviour. Amen.

To you, O Lord, we bring our lives,
troubled, broken or at ease
a sacrificial offering
for you to use.
Take away our selfishness
and teach us to love as you loved.
Take away our sense of pride
and show us the meaning of humility.
Take away our blindness
and show us the world through your eyes.
Take away our greed
and teach us how to give as you gave.
Show us your ways.
Teach us your paths
that we might walk with you more closely,
our hand in your hand,
our feet in your footsteps,
from the baby in a stable
to eternity, Amen.

FORGIVE us, Lord
we are a wandering people
who kneel before you now,
a people who bring prayers
and requests to your feet
when we have need of you
and nowhere else to turn,
then go our own way
when times are good
and life is easy.
Forgive us and draw us close;
teach us your way
that we might follow;
help us to walk in your company
and know your presence
from the moment we awake
until we lay our heads to rest. Amen

Gracious God, you have done so much for us
and we so little in return.
You ask for humility
and we are often a proud people;
you ask for willingness
and we are often a stubborn people;
you ask for repentance
and we are often a deaf people;
you ask for service
and we are often a busy people.
Gracious God, you want the best for us;
teach us obedience,
grant us forgiveness,
that we, like Mary
might be your willing servants. Amen.

GOD of the journey, your invitation is to all
to walk with you without fear of stumbling;
your arm enough to steady the feeblest soul;
your grace to rescue us should we fall.
Grant us faith enough to take you at your word,
to know that when our hearts are heavy
and the destination seems so distant
that you are there with us along the road.
Forgive us those times when we doubt your Word
when we awake and feel alone.

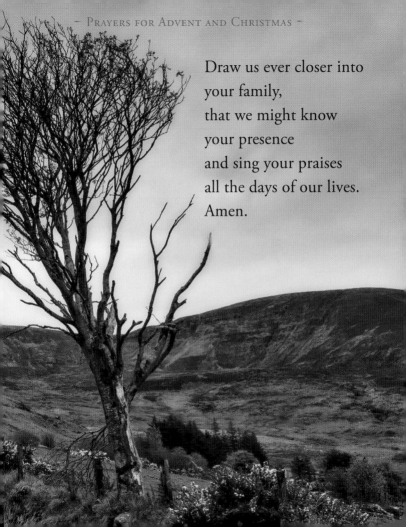

Draw us ever closer into
your family,
that we might know
your presence
and sing your praises
all the days of our lives.
Amen.

CREATOR God, you who love us more than we
can know,
who chose us from the very beginning to
be family,
we praise your holy name.
Jesus Christ, Son of God, Word become flesh,
who dwelt among us and was sacrificed for us,
we praise your holy name
Holy Spirit, presence and power in our lives,
from the moment that we first believed
we praise your holy name. Amen.

An Advent Prayer for Forgiveness and Mercy

FATHER,
we contemplate the birth of your Son.
He was born of the Virgin Mary
and came to live among us.
May we receive forgiveness and mercy
through Our Lord Jesus Christ, your Son,
who lives and reigns with you and the Holy Spirit,
one God, for ever and ever. Amen.

An Advent Prayer to Follow God's Will

GOD of love and mercy,
help us to follow the example of Mary,
always ready to do your will.
At the message of an angel
she welcomed your eternal Son
and, filled with the light of your Spirit,
she became the temple of your Word,
who lives and reigns with you and the Holy Spirit,
one God, for ever and ever. Amen.

An Advent Prayer to Grow in Love

FATHER in heaven,
our hearts desire the warmth of your love
and our minds are searching for the light of
your Word.
Increase our longing for Christ our Saviour
and give us the strength to grow in love,
that the dawn of his coming
may find us rejoicing in his presence
and welcoming the light of his truth.
We ask this in the name of Jesus the Lord. Amen.

An Old Advent Prayer to Jesus

You are our eternal salvation,
the unfailing light of the world.
Light everlasting,
you are truly our redemption.
Grieving that the human race was perishing
through the tempter's power,
without leaving the heights
you came to the depths in your loving kindness.
Readily taking our humanity by your gracious will,
you saved all earthly creatures, long since lost,
restoring joy to the world.
Redeem our souls and bodies, O Christ,
and so possess us as your shining dwellings.
By your first coming, make us righteous;
at your second coming, set us free:
So that, when the world is filled with light
and you judge all things, we may be clad in spotless robes
and follow in your steps, O King,
into the heavenly hall. Amen.

The Advent Wreath

The Advent wreath, marking the passing of the four
Sundays of Advent, is a lovely medieval tradition that
has come to us from Germany. Each Sunday another
candle is lit, together with the candles for the preceding
weeks. Advent wreaths are woven from evergreen leaves,
symbolising continuous life, while the circle of the
wreath represents endless life in God.

Lake Schluchsee in the
Black Forest, Germany, with
a giant Advent wreath.

Prayer while lighting the first
Advent candle:

STIR up thy power, O Lord, and come,
that by thy protection we may be rescued
from the dangers that beset us through our sins;
and be a Redeemer to deliver us;
Who lives and reigns with God the Father
in the unity of the Holy Spirit,
ever one God, world without end.

Prayer while lighting the second Advent candle:

STIR up our hearts, O Lord,
to prepare the paths of your Only-begotten Son:
that we may worthily serve you
with hearts purified by his coming:
Who lives and reigns with God the Father
in the unity of the Holy Spirit,
ever one God, world without end. Amen.

Prayer while lighting the third Advent candle:

WE beseech you to listen to our prayers, O Lord, and by the grace of your coming enlighten our darkened minds:
You who lives and reigns with God the Father in the unity of the Holy Spirit, one God for ever and ever. Amen.

Prayer while lighting the fourth Advent candle:

POUR forth your power, O Lord, and come:
Assist us by that mighty power,
so that by your grace and merciful kindness
we may swiftly receive the salvation that our sins
impede:
Who lives and reigns with you
in the unity of the Holy Spirit,
ever one God, world without end. Amen.

CHRISTMAS PRAYERS

LET Your goodness, Lord, appear to us, that we,
made in your image, conform ourselves to it.
In our own strength
we cannot imitate your majesty, power, and wonder
nor is it fitting for us to try.
But your mercy reaches from the heavens
through the clouds to the earth below.
You have come to us as a small child,
but you have brought us the greatest of all gifts,
the gift of eternal love
Caress us with your tiny hands,
embrace us with your tiny arms
and pierce our hearts with your soft, sweet cries.
Amen.

St Bernard of Clairvaux

LOVING Father, Help us remember the birth of
Jesus,
that we may share in the song of the angels,
the gladness of the shepherds,
and worship of the wise men.
Close the door of hate and open the door of love
all over the world. Let kindness come with every
gift and good desires with every greeting. Deliver
us from evil by the blessing which Christ brings,
and teach us to be merry with clear hearts.
May the Christmas morning make us happy to
be thy children, and Christmas evening bring us
to our beds with grateful thoughts, forgiving and
forgiven, for Jesus' sake. Amen.

Robert Louis Stevenson

O SWEET Child of Bethlehem,
grant that we may share with all our hearts
in this profound mystery of Christmas.
Put into the hearts of men and women this peace
for which they sometimes seek so desperately
and which you alone can give to them.
Help them to know one another better,
and to live as brothers and sisters,
children of the same Father.
Reveal to them also your beauty, holiness and
purity.
Awaken in their hearts
love and gratitude for your infinite goodness.
Join them all together in your love.
And give us your heavenly peace. Amen.

Pope John XXIII

LET the just rejoice,
for their justifier is born.
Let the sick and infirm rejoice,
For their saviour is born.
Let the captives rejoice,
For their Redeemer is born.
Let slaves rejoice,
for their Master is born.
Let free men rejoice,
For their Liberator is born.
Let All Christians rejoice,
For Jesus Christ is born.

St Augustine of Hippo

FATHER,
you make this holy night radiant
with the splendour of Jesus Christ our light.
We welcome him as Lord, true light of the world.
Bring us to eternal joy in the kingdom of heaven
where he lives and reigns with you and the
Holy Spirit, one God, for ever and ever. Amen.

GOD of love, Father of all,
the darkness that covered the earth
has given way to the bright dawn of your Word
made flesh.
Make us a people of this light.
Make us faithful to your Word
that we may bring your life to the waiting world.
Grant this through Christ our Lord. Amen.

LORD God,
we praise you for creating man,
and still more for restoring him in Christ.
Your Son shared our weakness:
may we share his glory,
for he lives and reigns with you and the Holy
Spirit, one God
for ever and ever. Amen.

GOD our Father,
you loved the world so much
you gave your only Son to free us
from the ancient power of sin and death.
Help us who wait for his coming
and lead us to true liberty.
We ask this through our Lord Jesus Christ,
your Son
who lives and reigns with you and the Holy Spirit,
one God, for ever and ever. Amen

PRAYERS FOR LENT AND EASTER

The forty days of Lent (not including Sundays), which begins on Ash Wednesday, mark a time of reflection and self-denial, in anticipation of the greatest season of all in the Christian year, Easter, which commemorates the resurrection of Jesus Christ.

PRAYERS DURING LENT

FATHER in Heaven,
the light of your truth bestows sight
to the darkness of sinful eyes.
May this season of repentance
bring us the blessing of your forgiveness
and the gift of your light.
Grant this through Christ our Lord. Amen.

O Lord,
The house of my soul is narrow;
enlarge it that you may enter in.
It is ruinous, O repair it!
It displeases Your sight.
I confess it, I know.
But who shall cleanse it,
to whom shall I cry but to you?
Cleanse me from my secret faults, O Lord,
and spare your servant from strange sins. Amen.

St Augustine of Hippo

O LORD, who hast mercy upon all,
take away from me my sins,
and mercifully kindle in me
the fire of thy Holy Spirit.
Take away from me the heart of stone,
and give me a heart of flesh,
a heart to love and adore Thee,
a heart to delight in Thee,
to follow and enjoy Thee, for Christ's sake, Amen.

St Ambrose of Milan

O my all-merciful God and Lord,
Jesus Christ, full of pity:
Through your great love you came down
and became incarnate in order to save everyone.
O Saviour, I ask you to save me by your grace!
If you save anyone because of their works,
that would not be grace but only reward of duty,
but you are compassionate and full of mercy!
You said, O my Christ,
'Whoever believes in me shall live and never die.'
If then, faith in you saves the lost, then save me,
O my God and Creator, for I believe.
Let faith and not my unworthy works be counted
to me, O my God,
for you will find no works which could account
me righteous.
O Lord, from now on let me love you as intensely
as I have loved sin,

and work for you as hard as I once worked for the evil one.

I promise that I will work to do your will,
my Lord and God, Jesus Christ, all the days of my life and for ever more. Amen.

St John Chrysostom

FATHER of light,
in you is found no shadow of change
but only the fullness of life and limitless truth.
Open our hearts to the voice of your Word
and free us from the original darkness
that shadows our vision.
Restore our sight that we may look upon Your Son
who calls us to repentance and a change of heart,
for he lives and reigns with you and the Holy Spirit,
one God, for ever and ever. Amen.

FATHER,
You have taught us to overcome our sins
by prayer, fasting and works of mercy.
When we are discouraged by our weakness,
give us confidence in your love.
We ask this through Our Lord Jesus Christ
your Son,
Who lives and reigns with you and the Holy Spirit
one God, for ever and ever. Amen.

The Stations of the Cross

The Stations of the Cross were devised by St Francis of Assisi in the 13th century. They can be said at any time of the year, but are traditional during Holy Week, especially on Good Friday. These stations are based on a scriptural version that was first celebrated by Pope John Paul II on Good Friday 1991. They would usually be led by a presiding minister, but this version can be prayed privately in church or at home.

Before each station:
WE adore you, O Christ, and we bless you, because by your holy cross you have redeemed the world

After each station:
LORD Jesus, help us walk in your steps.

First Station: Jesus in the Garden of Gethsemane
Then Jesus came with them to a place called Gethsemane, and he said to his disciples, 'Sit here while I go over there and pray.' He took along Peter and the two sons of Zebedee, and began to feel sorrow and

distress. Then he said to them, 'My soul is sorrowful
even to death. Remain here and keep watch with me.'
He advanced a little and fell prostrate in prayer, saying,
'My Father, if it is possible, let this cup pass from me;
yet, not as I will, but as you will.' When he returned to
his disciples he found them asleep. He said to Peter, 'So
you could not keep watch with me for one hour? Watch
and pray that you may not undergo the test. The spirit is
willing, but the flesh is weak.' *(Matthew 26:36–41)*

LORD, grant us your strength and wisdom,
that we may seek to follow your will in all things.

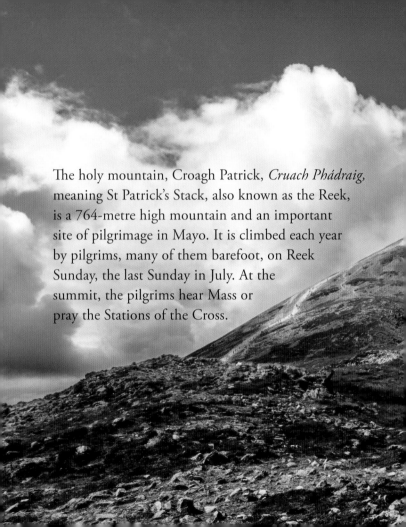

The holy mountain, Croagh Patrick, *Cruach Phádraig,*
meaning St Patrick's Stack, also known as the Reek,
is a 764-metre high mountain and an important
site of pilgrimage in Mayo. It is climbed each year
by pilgrims, many of them barefoot, on Reek
Sunday, the last Sunday in July. At the
summit, the pilgrims hear Mass or
pray the Stations of the Cross.

Second Station: Jesus, Betrayed by Judas, is Arrested.

Then, while [Jesus] was still speaking, Judas, one of the Twelve, arrived, accompanied by a crowd with swords and clubs, who had come from the chief priests, the scribes, and the elders. His betrayer had arranged a signal with them, saying, 'the man I shall kiss is the one; arrest him and lead him away securely.' He came and immediately went over to him and said, 'Rabbi.' And he kissed him. At this they laid hands on him and arrested him.

(Mark 14: 43–46)

LORD, grant us the courage of our convictions,
that our lives may faithfully reflect the good news
you bring.

The first station of the cross
on Croagh Patrick.

Third Station: Jesus is Condemned by the Sanhedrin.
When day came the council of elders of the people met,
both chief priests and scribes, and they brought him
before their Sanhedrin. They said, 'If you are the Messiah,
tell us,' but he replied to them, 'If I tell you, you will
not believe, and if I question, you will not respond. But
from this time on the Son of Man will be seated at the
right hand of the power of God.' They all asked, 'Are you
then the Son of God?' He replied to them, 'You say that
I am.' Then they said, 'What further need have we for
testimony? We have heard it from his own mouth.'
(Luke 22: 66–71)

LORD, grant us your sense of righteousness
that we may never cease to work
to bring about the justice of the kingdom that you
promised.

Fourth Station: Jesus is Denied by Peter.
Now Peter was sitting outside in the courtyard. One of
the maids came over to him and said, 'You too were with
Jesus the Galilean.' But he denied it in front of everyone,

saying, 'I do not know what you are talking about!' As he went out to the gate, another girl saw him and said to those who were there, 'This man was with Jesus the Nazarean.' Again he denied it with an oath, 'I do not know the man!' A little later the bystanders came over and said to Peter, 'Surely you too are one of them; even your speech gives you away.' At that he began to curse and to swear, 'I do not know the man.' And immediately a cock crowed. Then Peter remembered the word that Jesus had spoken: 'Before the cock crows you will deny me three times.' He went out and began to weep bitterly. *(Matthew 26: 69–75)*

LORD, grant us the gift of honesty
that we may not fear to speak the truth even when difficult.

Fifth Station: Jesus is Judged by Pilate.
The chief priests with the elders and the scribes, that is, the whole Sanhedrin, held a council. They bound Jesus, led him away, and handed him over to Pilate. Pilate questioned him, 'Are you the king of the Jews?' He said

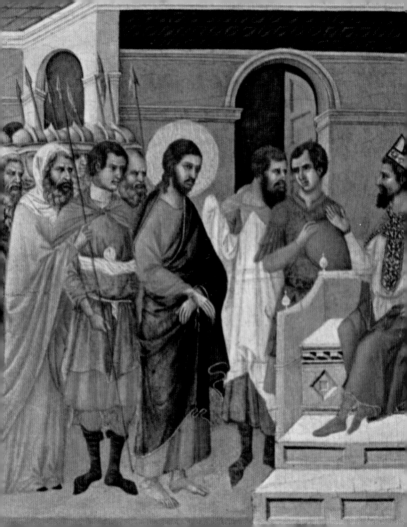

to him in reply, 'You say so.' The chief priests accused
him of many things. Again Pilate questioned him, 'Have
you no answer? See how many things they accuse you
of.' Jesus gave him no further answer, so that Pilate was
amazed … Pilate, wishing to satisfy the crowd, released
Barrabas … [and] handed [Jesus] over to be crucified.
(Mark 15: 1–5, 15)

LORD, grant us discernment
that we may see as you see, not as the world sees.

Sixth Station: Jesus is Scourged and Crowned with Thorns

Then Pilate took Jesus and had him scourged. And the
soldiers wove a crown out of thorns and placed it on
his head, and clothed him in a purple cloak, and they
came to him and said, 'Hail, King of the Jews!' And they
struck him repeatedly.
(John 19: 1–3)

Lord, grant us patience in times of suffering
that we may offer our lives as a sacrifice of praise.

Seventh Station: Jesus Bears the Cross.

When the chief priests and the guards saw [Jesus] they
cried out, 'Crucify him, crucify him!' Pilate said to them,
'Take him yourselves and crucify him. I find no guilt
in him.' ... They cried out, 'Take him away, take him
away! Crucify him!' Pilate said to them, 'Shall I crucify
your king?' The chief priests answered, 'We have no
king but Caesar.' Then he handed him over to them to
be crucified. So they took Jesus, and carrying the cross
himself he went out to what is called the Place of the
Skull, in Hebrew, Golgotha.
(John 19: 6, 15–17)

Lord, grant us strength of purpose
that we may faithfully bear our crosses each day.

Eighth Station: Jesus is Helped by Simon the Cyrenian to Carry the Cross.

They pressed into service a passer-by, Simon, a Cyrenian, who was coming in from the country, the father of Alexander and Rufus, to carry his cross.
(Mark 15: 21)

LORD, grant us willing spirits
that we may be your instruments on earth.

Ninth Station: Jesus Meets the Women of Jerusalem.

A large crowd of people followed Jesus, including many women who mourned and lamented him. Jesus turned to them and said, 'Daughters of Jerusalem, do not weep for me; weep instead for yourselves and for your children, for indeed, the days are coming when people will say, "Blessed are the barren, the wombs that never bore and the breasts that never nursed." At that time, people will say to the mountains, "Fall upon us!" and to the hills, "Cover us!" for if these things are done when the wood is green what will happen when it is dry?'
(Luke 23: 27–31)

Lord, grant us gentle spirits
that we may comfort those who mourn.

Tenth Station: Jesus is Crucified.
When they came to the place called the Skull, they
crucified him and the criminals there, one on his right,
the other on his left. [Then Jesus said, 'Father, forgive
them, they know not what they do.']
(Luke 23: 33–34)

Lord, grant us merciful hearts
that we may bring your reconciliation and forgiveness
to all.

**Eleventh Station: Jesus Promises his Kingdom to the
Good Thief.**
Now one of the criminals hanging there reviled Jesus,
saying, 'Are you not the Messiah? Save yourself and us.'
The other, however, rebuking him, said in reply, 'Have
you no fear of God, for you are subject to the same
condemnation? And indeed, we have been condemned
justly, for the sentence we received corresponds to our

crimes, but this man has done nothing criminal.' Then he said, 'Jesus, remember me when you come into your kingdom.' He replied to him, 'Amen, I say to you, today you will be with me in Paradise.'
(Luke 23: 39–43)

Lord, grant us perseverance
that we may never stop seeking you.

Twelfth Station: Jesus Speaks to His Mother and the Disciple.

Standing by the cross of Jesus were his mother and his mother's sister, Mary the wife of Clopas, and Mary of Magdala. When Jesus saw his mother and the disciple there whom he loved, he said to his mother, 'Woman, behold, your son.' Then he said to the disciple, 'Behold, your mother.' And from that hour the disciple took her into his home.
(John 19: 25–27)

Lord, grant us constancy
that we may be willing to stand by those in need.

Thirteenth Station: Jesus Dies on the Cross.
It was now about noon and darkness came over the
whole land until three in the afternoon because of an
eclipse of the sun. Then the veil of the temple was torn
down the middle. Jesus cried out in a loud voice, 'Father,
into your hands I commend my spirit'; and when he had
said this he breathed his last.
(Luke 23: 44–46)

LORD, grant us trust in you
that when our time on earth in ended
our spirits may come to you without delay.

Fourteenth Station: Jesus is Placed in the Tomb.
When it was evening, there came a rich man from
Arimathea named Joseph, who was himself a disciple of
Jesus. He went to Pilate and asked for the body of Jesus;
then Pilate ordered it to be handed over. Taking the
body, Joseph wrapped it [in] clean linen and laid it in his
new tomb that he had hewn in the rock. Then he rolled a
huge stone across the entrance to the tomb and departed.
(Matthew 27: 57–60)

Lord, grant us your compassion
that we may always provide for those in need.

Closing Prayer:

LORD Jesus Christ,
your passion and death is the sacrifice
that unites earth and heaven
and reconciles all people to you.
May we who have faithfully reflected
on these mysteries
follow in your steps and so come to
share your glory in heaven
where you live and reign with the
Father and the Holy Spirit
one God, for ever and ever. Amen.

PRAYERS AT EASTERTIME

When our faith
stands at the grave,
grieving
for a stone that's rolled away,
forgive us.

When our faith,
beset by doubt, sees
no further
than an empty tomb today,
forgive us.

Bring to mind
the cry of Mary,
'I have seen the Lord!'
and grant us faith to believe. Amen.

Lord, we thank you
that Easter is not about
a people,
but all people,
that your love
and your Salvation
are for all who confess
with voices, hearts and lives
that the tomb is empty
because Jesus is risen,
that we might know
forgiveness,
that lives might be
reborn
and your name
glorified
now and for eternity. Amen.

EASTER reminds us
that each time
we deny you, Lord,
another nail is sharpened;
and each time
we defy you, Lord,
into your hand it's hammered.
When faith is weak,
temptation strong
and courage fails,
forgive us, Lord,
and once again
become that risen presence
within our hearts. Amen.

GOD of Promise and God of Hope,
who through your great mercy
have granted us new birth
through the death and resurrection of Jesus Christ,
we praise your wonderful name!
God of Glory and God of Might,
who through your great power
have granted us new strength
to endure all things through faith in Christ our
risen King,
we praise your wonderful name! Amen.

WE are often not the Easter People
that we should be,
living in the certain knowledge
of your great mercy and love.
Distracted by the world around us
we fail to hear your voice,
or hide when faith is challenged
as we wander off the path.
Forgive us, we pray;
restore the love that we first had,
a faith that can endure.
We will keep our eyes fixed on you, Lord,
and with you at our right hand
we shall not be shaken. Amen.

God so loved the world that he gave his only Son
for the sake of me
and you
and other sinners too.
God so loved the world.
Blessed are you Lord Jesus, our Saviour and
Redeemer. Amen.

How often when weary
do we sigh 'The spirit is willing,
but the body is weak.'
How often when in prayer
are thoughts distracted by
sounds or circumstance,
or prayers diverted
by trivial concerns.
Baggage carried with us
rather than left at your feet.
How often do we find ourselves
apologising to you,
for our abbreviated prayer life.
And yet you draw us still
to be in your presence,
as you did the disciples at Gethsemane.

You want us to share in your life,
to play our part.
You told your disciples to watch and pray
so that they might not fall into temptation.
Do you ask the same of us
and do we also fail you,
each time we whisper
'The spirit is willing,
but the body is weak'?
Grant us the strength, Lord,
of body and of spirit,
to offer you the sacrifice
of our lives. Amen.

IT is only right,
with all the powers of our heart and mind,
to praise you, Father
and your only-begotten Son,
Our Lord Jesus Christ:
Dear Father, by your wondrous
condescension of loving-kindness toward us,
your servants, you gave up your Son.
Dear Jesus, you paid the debt of Adam
for us to the Eternal Father by
your Blood poured
forth in loving-kindness.
You cleared away the darkness of sin
By your magnificent and radiant Resurrection.
You broke the bonds of death
and rose from the grave as a Conqueror.
You reconciled heaven and earth.

Our life had no hope of eternal happiness
before you redeemed us.
Your Resurrection has washed away our sins,
restored our innocence and brought us joy.
How inestimable is the tenderness
of your love! Amen.

St Gregory the Great

CHRIST is Risen: The world below lies desolate.

Christ is Risen: The spirits of evil are fallen.

Christ is Risen: The angels of God are rejoicing.

Christ is Risen: The tombs of the dead are empty.

Christ is Risen indeed from the dead,
the first of the sleepers.

Glory and power are his forever and ever. Amen.

St Hippolytus of Rome

GOD our Father,
by raising Christ your Son
you conquered the power of death
and opened for us the way to eternal life.
Let our celebration today
raise us up and renew our lives
by the Spirit that is within us.
Grant this through our Lord Jesus Christ, your
Son,
who lives and reigns with you and Holy Spirit,
one God, for ever and ever. Amen.

GOD and Father of our Lord Jesus Christ,
though your people walk in the valley of darkness,
no evil should they fear;
for they follow in faith the call of the shepherd
whom you have sent for their hope and strength.
Attune our minds to the sound of his voice,
lead our steps in the path he has shown,
that we may know the strength of his outstretched
arm and enjoy the light of your presence for ever.
We ask this through Christ our Lord. Amen.

GOD our Father,
may we look forward with hope
to our resurrection,
for you have made us your sons and daughters,
and restored the joy of our youth.
We ask this through our Lord Jesus Christ, your
Son,who lives and reigns with you and the Holy
Spirit, one God, for ever and ever. Amen.

ALMIGHTY and ever-living God,
give us new strength
from the courage of Christ our shepherd,
and lead us to join the saints in heaven,
where he lives and reigns with you and the Holy
Spirit, one God, for ever and ever. Amen.

GOD of mercy,
you wash away our sins in water,
you give us a new birth in the Spirit,
and redeem us in the blood of Christ.
As we celebrate Christ's resurrection,
increase our awareness of these blessings,
and renew your gift of life within us.
We ask this through our Lord Jesus Christ, your
Son, who lives and reigns with you and the Holy
Spirit, one God, for ever and ever. Amen.

Draw us forth, God of all creation.
Draw us forward and away from limited certainty
into the immense world of your love.
Give us the capacity to even for a moment
taste the richness of the feast you give us.
Give us the peace to live with uncertainty,
with questions, with doubts.
Help us to experience the resurrection anew
with open wonder and an increasing ability
to see you in the people of Easter. Amen.

MAY the glory
and the promise
of this joyous time of year
bring peace
and happiness to you
and those you hold most dear.

And may Christ,
Our Risen Saviour,
always be there by your side
to bless you
most abundantly
and be your loving guide. Amen.

PRAYERS FOR THE DYING AND BEREAVED

Praying with and for someone who is dying can bring comfort to all involved. The prayers can be as simple as the Our Father, Hail Mary or the Rosary, or you could pray some of the prayers on the following pages.

PRAYERS WITH THE DYING

These prayers can be recited with the dying person, alternating with periods of silence. You can repeat the same prayers as often as wished.

John 6:37–40
EVERYTHING that the Father gives me will come to me,
and anyone who comes to me I will never drive away;
for I have come down from heaven, not to do my own
will, but the will of him who sent me.
And this is the will of him who sent me,
that I should lose nothing of all that he has given me,
but raise it up on the last day.
This is indeed the will of my Father,
that all who see the Son and believe in him
may have eternal life;
and I will raise them up on the last day.

Psalm 23
The Lord is my shepherd, I shall not want.
He makes me lie down in green pastures;
he leads me beside still waters;
he restores my soul.
He leads me in right paths for his name's sake.

Even though I walk through the darkest valley,
I fear no evil; for you are with me;
your rod and your staff –
they comfort me.

You prepare a table before me
in the presence of my enemies;
you anoint my head with oil; my cup overflows.
Surely goodness and mercy shall follow me
all the days of my life,
and I shall dwell in the house of the LORD
my whole life long.

Nunc Dimittis (Luke 2:29–32)

Master, now you are dismissing your servant in
peace, according to your word;
for my eyes have seen your salvation, which you
have prepared in the presence of all peoples,
a light for revelation to the Gentiles
and for glory to your people Israel.

Psalm 121

I LIFT up my eyes to the hills –
from where will my help come?
My help comes from the LORD,
who made heaven and earth.

He will not let your foot be moved;
he who keeps you will not slumber.
He who keeps Israel
will neither slumber nor sleep.

The LORD is your keeper;
the LORD is your shade at your right hand.
The sun shall not strike you by day,
nor the moon by night.

The LORD will keep you from all evil;
he will keep your life.
The LORD will keep your going out and your coming in
from this time on and for evermore.
Both now and for ever.

As the time of death approaches

Prayer of Commendation

Go forth, Christian soul, from this world
in the name of God the almighty Father,
who created you,
in the name of Jesus Christ, Son of the living God,
who suffered for you,
in the name of the Holy Spirit, who was poured
out upon you, go forth, faithful Christian.
May you live in peace this day,
may your home be with God in Zion,
with Mary, the Virgin Mother of God,
with Joseph, and all the Angels and Saints. Amen.

PRAYERS AFTER DEATH

Prayer for the Dead

In your hands, O Lord,
we humbly entrust our brothers and sisters.
In this life you embraced them with your tender love;
deliver them now from every evil
and bid them eternal rest.
The old order has passed away:
welcome them into paradise,
where there will be no sorrow, no weeping or pain, but
fullness of peace and joy
with your Son and the Holy Spirit
for ever and ever. Amen.

Eternal rest grant unto (*name*) O Lord,
and let perpetual light shine upon them.
May they rest in peace.
May their souls and the souls of all the faithful departed,
through the mercy of God, rest in peace. Amen.

Prayers Immediately after Death

The following prayers may be recited immediately after death and may be repeated in the hours that follow.

SAINTS of God, come to *his/her* aid!
Come to meet *him/her*, Angels of the Lord!
Receive *his/her* soul and present *him/her* to God the Most High.
May Christ, who called you, take you to himself; may Angels lead you to Abraham's side.
Give *him/her* eternal rest, O Lord,
and may your light shine on *him/her* forever.
Let us pray.
All-powerful and merciful God,
we commend to you (*name*), your servant. In your mercy and love,
blot out the sins *he/she* has committed through human weakness.
In this world *he/she* has died:
let *him/her* live with you forever. Through Christ our Lord. Amen

ETERNAL rest grant unto *him/her*, O Lord.
And let perpetual light shine upon *him/her*.
May *he/she* rest in peace.
Amen.

MAY *his/her* soul and the souls of all the faithful departed,
through the mercy of God, rest in peace. Amen.

LORD, welcome into your calm and peaceful kingdom
those who have departed out of this present life to be
with you.
Grant them rest and a place with the spirits of the just;
and give them the life that shows no age, the reward that
passes not away.
Through Christ Our Lord. Amen.

St Ignatius Loyola

PRAYERS FOR MOURNERS

LORD God, you are attentive to the voice of our pleading. Let us find in your Son comfort in our sadness, certainty in our doubt, and courage to live through this hour. Make our faith strong through Christ our Lord. Amen.

LORD, (*name*) is gone now from this earthly dwelling, and has left behind those who mourn *his/her* absence. Grant that we may hold *his/her* memory dear, never bitter for what we have lost nor in regret for the past, but always in hope of the eternal Kingdom where you will bring us together again. Through Christ our Lord. Amen.

MAY the love of God and the peace of the Lord Jesus Christ bless and console us and gently wipe every tear from our eyes: in the name of the Father, and of the Son, and of the Holy Spirit. Amen.

For Those Mourning the Death of a Child

O Lord, whose ways are beyond understanding, listen to the prayers of your faithful people: that those weighed down by grief at the loss of this little child may find reassurance in your infinite goodness. Through Christ our Lord. Amen.

PRAYERS AT THE GRAVESIDE

LORD Jesus Christ, by your own three days in the tomb, you hallowed the graves of all who believe in you and so made the grave a sign of hope that promises resurrection even as it claims our mortal bodies. Grant that our *brother/sister (name)* may sleep here in peace until you awaken *him/her* to glory, for you are the resurrection and the life. Then *he/she* will see you face to face and in your light will see light and know the splendour of God, for you live and reign for ever and ever. Amen.

O GOD, by whose mercy the faithful departed find rest, send your holy Angel to watch over this grave. Through Christ our Lord. Amen

Chapter 7

BLESSINGS FOR ALL OCCASIONS

Blessings are commonplace in
Ireland, where even greetings
take the form of blessings.

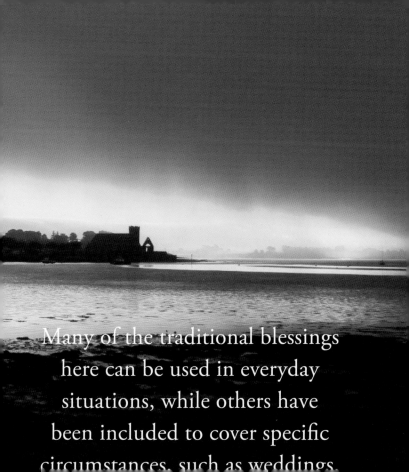

Many of the traditional blessings
here can be used in everyday
situations, while others have
been included to cover specific
circumstances, such as weddings,

MAY the road rise up to meet you,
and may the wind be always at
your back.
May the sun shine warm upon
your face,
and the rain fall soft upon
your fields.
And until we meet again,
may God hold you in the palm
of his hand.

MAY your troubles be less
and your blessings be more
and may nothing but happiness
come through your door.

MAY the Lord bless you and
keep you.
May the Lord's face shine
upon you and be gracious to
you.
May the Lord turn his face to
you and bring you peace.

MAY God bless the
ground you walk on.

MAY you see God's light on
the path ahead
when the road you walk is dark.
May you always hear,
even in your hour of sorrow,
the gentle singing of the lark.
When times are hard may hardness
never turn your heart to stone,
May you always remember
when the shadows fall –
you do not walk alone.

Deep peace of the running wave
to you.
Deep peace of the flowing air to you.
Deep peace of the quiet earth to you.
Deep peace of the shining stars
to you.
May the beauties of the earth and sky
and sea
fill your heart with lasting peace and
contentment.

MAY your days be many
and your troubles few.
May all God's blessings descend
on you.
May peace be within you,
may your hearts be strong,
and may you find what you're seeking,
wherever you roam.

MAY God give you,
for every storm a rainbow,
for every tear a smile,
for every care a promise,
and a blessing in each trial.
For every problem life sends,
a faithful friend to share,
for every sigh, a sweet song,
and an answer for each prayer.

MAY you always have work for your
hands to do.
May your pockets hold always a coin
or two.
May the sun shine bright on your
window pane.
May the rainbow be certain to follow
each rain.
May the hand of a friend always be
near you.
And may God fill your heart with
gladness to cheer you.

MAY you be blessed
with warmth in your home,
love in your heart,
peace in your soul,
and joy your whole life through.

MAY God put luck on you.

Go gcuire Dia an t-ádh ort.

MAY the peace of God enfold us,
the love of God uphold us,
the wisdom of God control us.

MAY the peace of God reign in
this place
and the love of God forever hold
you tight.
May the Spirit of God flow through
your life
and the joy of God uphold you day
and night.

LET the majesty of the Father
be the light by which you walk,
the compassion of the Son
be the love by which you walk,
the presence of the Spirit
be the power by which you walk.

THE love of God be the passion
in your heart.
The joy of God your strength
when times are hard.
The presence of God a peace
that overflows.
The Word of God the seed
that you might sow.

THE peace of God be in your heart.
The grace of God be in your words.
The love of God be in your hands.
The joy of God be in your soul
and in the song that your life sings.

God's love surround you, God's
Spirit guide you,
God's whisper cheer you, God's
peace calm you,
God's shield protect you, God's
wisdom arm you,
wherever God may lead you.

THE embrace of the Father
be the comfort you desire.
The name of the Son
be the one on whom you rely.
The presence of the Spirit
be with you every hour.
The Three in One
be the focus of all you are.

May your day be blessed
by moments of quietness,
light in your darkness,
strength in your weakness,
grace in your meekness,
joy in your gladness,
peace in your stillness.
May your day be blessed.

MAY the Lord bless you.
May he preserve you and turn his face
towards you.
May he have mercy on you and give
you his peace.
May he show you always his divine
glory and give you his holy approval.

St Francis of Assisi

MAY the love of the Father,
the tenderness of the Son,
and the presence of the Spirit,
gladden your heart
and bring peace to your soul,
this day and all days.

GOD bless the corners of this house
and be the lintel blessed.
Bless the hearth, the table too,
and bless each place of rest.
Bless each door that opens wide
to stranger, kith and kin;
Bless each shining window pane
that lets the sunshine in.
Bless the roof beams up above,
bless every solid wall.
The peace of Man, the peace of love,
the peace of God on all.

BLESS the house wherein you live,
bless every window, wall and door.
Bless everyone beneath its roof
and every hand that works to keep all
safe within.

MAY Brigid bless the house in which
you live,
bless every fireside, every wall and
door,
bless every heart that beats beneath
this roof,
and every hand that works to bring
you joy,
and every foot that walks over its
threshold.
May Brigid bless the house that
shelters you.

BLESS this house, O Lord, we pray.
Make it safe by night and day.
Bless these walls so firm and stout,
keeping want and trouble out.
Bless the roof and chimney tall,
let thy peace lie over all.
Bless the doors that they may prove
ever open to joy and love.
Bless the windows shining bright,
letting in God's heavenly light.
Bless the hearth a-blazing there,
with smoke ascending like a prayer.
Bless the people here within,
keep them pure and free from sin.
Bless us all, that one day, we
May be fit, O Lord, to dwell with thee.

May God the Father
prepare your journey,
Jesus the Son
guide your footsteps,
the Spirit of Life
strengthen your body,
the Three in One
watch over you,
on every road
that you may follow.

UNTIL we meet again,
may God hold you
in the palm of his hand.

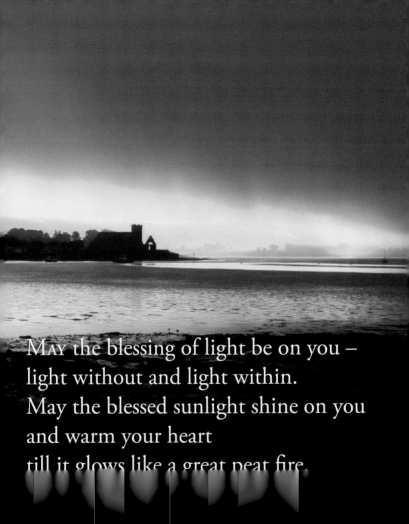

May the blessing of light be on you –
light without and light within.
May the blessed sunlight shine on you
and warm your heart
till it glows like a great peat fire.

LET nothing disturb you,
let nothing frighten you.
All things are passing away:
God never changes.
Patience obtains all things.
Whoever has God lacks nothing;
God alone suffices.

St Teresa of Avila

A Blessing for Baptism

DEAREST Father in Heaven,
Bless this child and bless this day
Of new beginnings.
Smile upon this child
And surround this child, Lord,
With the soft mantle of your love.
Teach this child to follow in your
footsteps,
And to live life in the ways of
Love, faith, hope and charity.

Wedding Blessings

MAY luck be your companion,
May friends stay by your side.
May God bless you with happiness
And love and faith abide.

MAY God bless you with everything
you need,
Some things that you want
and all the people that will support
and love you.

MAY God be with you and
bless you.
May you see your children's
children.
May you be poor in misfortune
And rich in blessings,
And may you have nothing
but happiness
From this day forward.

MAY your mornings bring joy and your
evenings bring peace.
May your troubles grow few as your
blessings increase.
May the saddest day of your future
be no worse than the happiest day of
your past.
May your hands be forever clasped in
friendship
and your hearts joined for ever in love.
Your lives are very special,
God has touched you in many ways.
May his blessings rest upon you
and fill all your coming days.

Funeral Blessings

MAY *his/her* soul be at the right
hand of God.
Ar dheis Dé go raibh a anam.

MAY God level the road
for *his/her* soul.

MAY God never
weaken you.
Nár laga Dia thú.

MAY the light of the sun of God
shine on *his/her* soul.
Solas Mhic Dé ar a n-anam.

Picture credits

p1 James Fraser/Shutterstock

p3 Memorial Cross in Kildownet Cemetery overlooking Achill Sound and the Corraun Peninsula, Achill Island, County Mayo, George Munday/Alamy

p5 19th C print, Teapot Press

p10 *High Mass at a Fishing Village on the Zuyder Zee*, Holland, 1876, Alamy

p13 Rihardz/Shutterstock

p14 *God the Father*, Cima da Conegliano/Alamy

p17 *La Orana Maria* (Hail Mary), Paul Gauguin, 1891, Google Art Project

p19 *Exhortation of the Apostles*, 1886–94, James Tissot (1836–1902), Brooklyn Museum/Wiki

p20 A Woman Kneels in Prayer at White Cross and Statue at Sheep's Head near Ahakista, County Cork, Design Pics Inc/Alamy Stock Photo

p23 *Guardian Angel*, Jose Ignacio Cobo Y Guzman (1666–1746), Peter Horree/Alamy

p24 Stained-glass window in the Church of the Nativity of the Blessed Virgin Mary at Timoleague, Harry Clarke/Alamy

p29 Basilica of Our Lady of Knock, National Shrine of Our Lady, Knock, Thoom/Shutterstock

p31 Small prayer note *Notre Dame de Lourdes, Marian apparition*, Lourdes, 1858, France, c. 1895 Interphoto/Alamy

p33 *Virgin and Child in Glory: Salve Regina*. Sforza Hours. Milan, circa 1490; Flemish insertions, 1517–20, Gerard Horenbout/Alamy

p35 *Portrait miniature of John Henry Newman*, William Charles Ross, 19th C engraving, coloured 2020, Teapot Press

p37 *Mother Most Amiable, Litany of Loreto*, Ezio Annichini, early 20th C, Collection Royal School of Needlework, London

p41 *The Angelus*, (1857–59), Jean-François Millet, Wiki/Musée d'Orsay

p44 Ruggiero Scardigno/Shutterstock

p45 *The Fisherman's Mother*, Helen Mabel Trevor (1831–1900), National Gallery of Ireland

p49 *The Fifteen Mysteries and the Virgin of the Rosary*, possibly Goswijn van der Weyden, (c.1491–1538), Wikipedia

p50 *Gabrielle d'Arjuzon praying for the recovery of her mother's health*, 1813–14, Philippe Coupin (1773–1851), Alamy

p54 Zlonimir Atlectic/Shutterstock

p57 *Saint Brendan the Navigator*, 13th-century manuscript, HeritagePics/Alamy

p58 Oixxo/Shutterstock

p59 Stained glass in Catholic church in Dublin depicting St Brigid of Kildare, Jurand/Shutterstock

p61 St Bridgid's Day crosses made out of rushes, Mari/Alamy

p62 Saint Anthony of Padua, Raphael, c. 1502. Incamerastock / Alamy

p65 Woodcut print with hand-colouring of St Christopher from Buxheim on the Upper Rhine, 1423, Wikipedia

p67 *St Clare of Assisi*, Simone Martini (1284–1344), Wikipedia

p68 Peter Crocka/Shutterstock

p70 *St Columba*, Harry Clarke, 1936-37, St Columba's church, Perth, Australia, Jeremy Storey

~ PICTURE CREDITS ~

p73 *Saint Francis Receiving the Stigmata*, 1590–95, El Greco (1541–1614), National Gallery of Ireland

p75 Stone floral mosaic with the St Francis playing the violin for the birds in side chapel of Basilica di Santa Maria in Aracoeli, unknown artist. Renata Sedmakova/Shutterstock

p76 St Francis Xavier, from an illustration in *History of the Church*, circa 1880, Sergey Kogl/Shutterstock

p79 St Gerard Majella, 19th C print, Teapot Press

p80 *The portrait of St John XXIII*, Karlskirche, Clemens Fuchs, Renata Sedmakova/Shutterstock.

p83 *Cardinal John Henry Newman (1801–1890)*, Sir John Everett Millais, 1881, Pictorial Press Ltd/Alamy

p84 Pope John Paul II: Visit to Ireland. May 1981, Trinity Mirror/Mirrorpix/Alamy

p86 *St Joseph with Infant Christ in his Arms*, Guido Reni (1575–1642), Wikipedia

p89 *St Jude the Apostle*, Anthony Van Dyck, Art History Museum, Vienna Album/Alamy

p90 Glendalough Monastery St. Kevin's Church Derrybawn, Glendalough, Co. Wicklow, Marko Bablitz/Shutterstock

p92 Mulhall Photos/Shutterstock

p95 *The Deposition*, 1507, Raphael, showing a distressed, reddish-blonde Mary Magdalene dressed in fine clothes clutching the hand of Jesus' body as he is carried to the tomb, Wikipedia

p97 *The Archangel Michael and St Dominic and S. Francis and Jesus the Pantokrator in Chiesa di San Domenico*, Giacomo Francia (1486–1557), Renata Sedmakova/Shutterstock

p99 *St Oliver Plunkett*, Garrett Morphey; Edward Lutterell Medium, 1681, National Portrait Gallery, London

p100 St Patrick journeying to Tara to convert the Irish to Christianity in the 5th century AD. Hand-coloured halftone of an illustration, North Wind Picture Archives/Alamy

p102 The Rock of Cashel, County Tipperary, M. Reel/Shutterstock

p105 Mother Teresa, Belfast, PA Images/Alamy

p106 Thérèse of Lisieux, Wikipedia

p107 *St Teresa of the Child Jesus,* Church of St George, Lyon, France, Godong/Alamy

p108 *Vincent de Paul*, Simon François de Tours (1606-1671), Mission des Lazaristes, Paris, France, Wikipedia

p110 *Adoration of the Shepherds*, Giuseppe Bartolomeo Chiari (1654–1727), Ian Dagnall Computing/Alamy

p116 Mountain road with wind-blown lone tree in the Comeragh Mountains, Tipperary, Shutterstock

p119 Painted divine figure, Church of San Sebastiano, Rome, Robodread/Alamy

p123 *The Finding of the Saviour in the Temple*, William Holman Hunt, Google Art Project

p125 *Adoration of the Shepherds (The Light of the World)*, 1750, Francois Boucher (1703–1770), Peter Horree/Alamy

p126 Lake Schluchsee in the Black Forest, Germany, with giant advent wreath, Matgo/Shutterstock

p128 Bean Images/Shutterstock

p133 Van Reel/Shutterstock

p136 *Advent and Triumph of Christ*, 1480, Hans Memling, Alte Pinakothek, Munich, Germany, Ivan Vdovin/Alamy

p139 *Adoration of the Shepherds*, Girolamo Troppa (1630–after 1710), National Gallery of Ireland

255